D0772394

Staying Safe in Emergencies

by Robin Nelson

Series consultants: Sonja Green, MD, and
Distinguished Professor Emerita Ann Nolte, PhD,
Department of Health Sciences, Illinois State University

Lerner Publications Company • Minneapolis

Lerner Publications Company
A division of Lerner Publishing Group
241 First Avenue North
Minneapolis, MN 55401 USA

Website address: www.lernerbooks.com

Words in **bold type** are explained in a glossary on page 31.

Library of Congress Cataloging-in-Publication Data

Nelson, Robin, 1971–
     Staying safe in emergencies / by Robin Nelson.
        p. cm. – (Pull ahead books)
     Includes index.
     ISBN-13: 978-0-8225-3391-7 (lib. bdg. : alk. paper)
     ISBN-10: 0-8225-3391-X (lib. bdg. : alk. paper)
     1. Children—Health and hygiene—Juvenile literature. 2.
Health risk assessment—Juvenile literature. 3. Safety
education—Juvenile literature. 4. Emergency medical
services—Juvenile literature. 5. Self-care, Health—Juvenile
literature. I. Title. II.Series.
RJ370.N45 2006
613'.0432–dc22   2005023584

Manufactured in the United States of America
1 2 3 4 5 6 – JR – 11 10 09 08 07 06

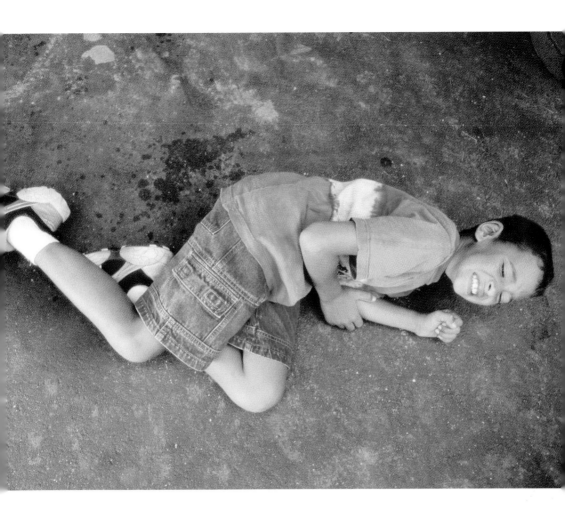

Help! **Emergency!**

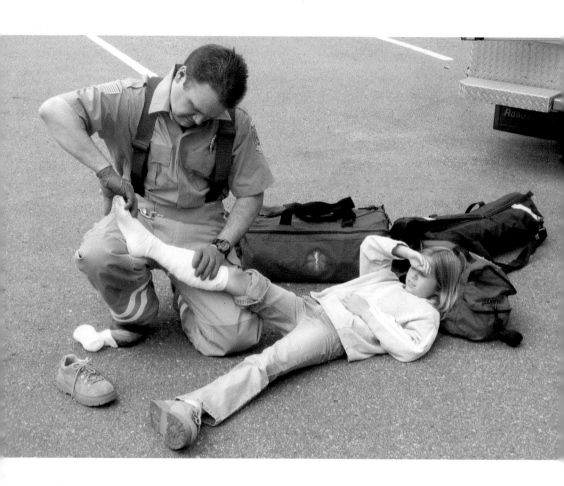

An emergency is when someone is
badly hurt or in danger.

It is an emergency when someone is bleeding a lot or has a broken bone. When someone can't breathe well or is **unconscious,** it is an emergency.

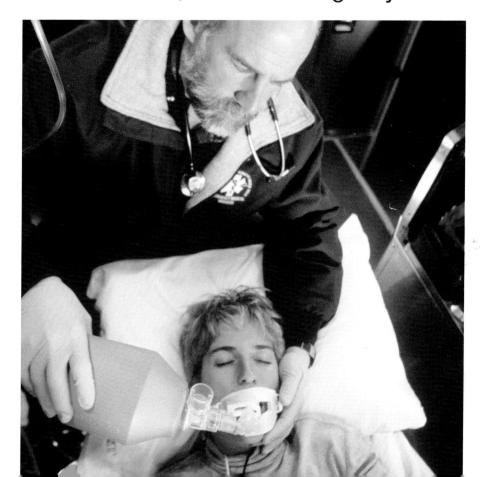

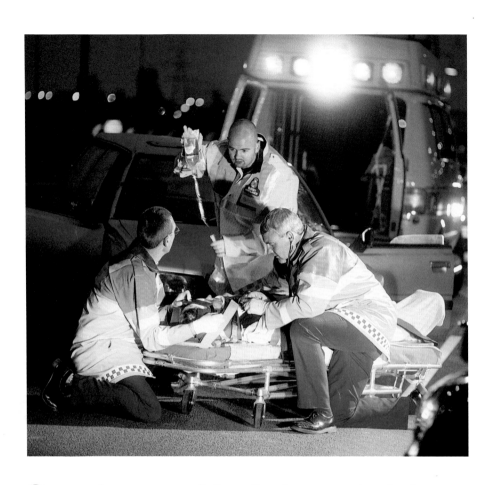

Sometimes **accidents** happen. It is
important to be ready.

Do you know what to do in an emergency?

Try to stay calm. Find an adult or yell for help.

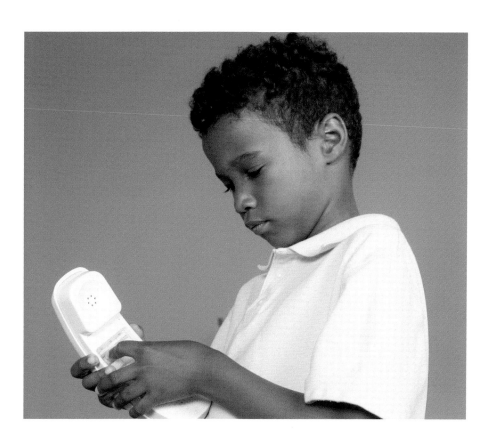

If an adult is not near, you can
telephone for help. Do you know how?
Dial 911.

The person who answers a 911 call will ask you your name. He or she will ask what happened and where you are. Be sure to speak clearly and slowly.

The person on the phone will send the police, the fire department, or an **ambulance.** Stay on the phone until help arrives.

Should you call 911 if you fall off your bike and scrape your knee? No, a scraped knee is not an emergency. Instead, find an adult to help you.

Call 911 only in an emergency. Are you not sure if something is an emergency? It is better to be safe and call 911.

Fire! What should you do? Get
outside right away! Call 911 from a
neighbor's house.

If your clothes are on fire, remember
"stop, drop, and roll!" Stop right away,
drop to the floor, and start to roll. This
puts out the fire.

There are
ways you
can help
when
someone
gets hurt.

Learning **first aid** can help you take care of simple **injuries.** What are some ways to give first aid?

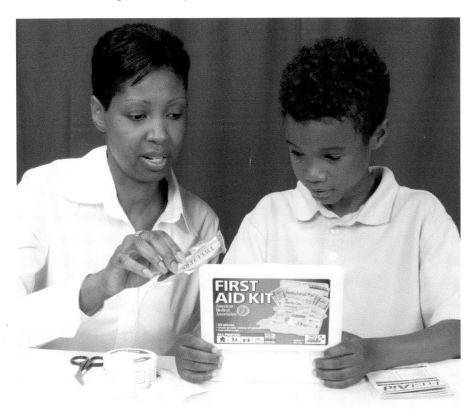

Ouch! Matt cut his finger. It is bleeding. What should you do?

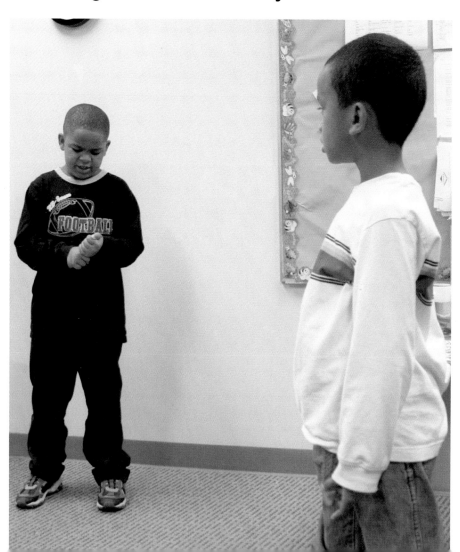

Yell for help. Get a clean cloth. Press the cloth on the cut. Keep pressing until the bleeding stops or until help comes.

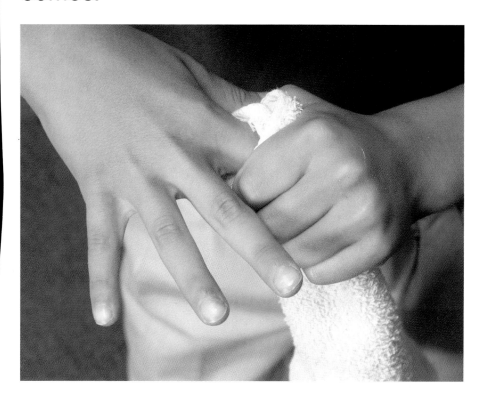

Ouch! Maggie touched a hot pot on the stove. She burned her hand. It is turning red. What should you do?

Turn on the cold water in the sink.
Have Maggie put her hand in the cold
water. Her hand will feel better. Go
find an adult to help.

Megan fell down and hurt her arm! She can't move it. What should you do?

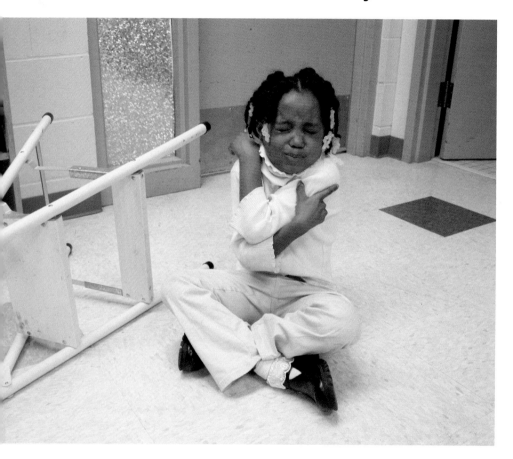

Tell Megan not to move. If her arm is
broken, moving it will make it worse.
Run to get an adult to help.

Oh, no! Tommy ate something from the medicine shelf. It could be **poisonous.** What should you do?

Take the
bottle away.
Call 911.

How else can you be ready? Practice what to do in emergencies. Make a first aid kit. Keep a list of important numbers near the phone.

EMERGENCY	911
Dr. Johnson	953-789-5555
Poison Control	1-800-222-1222
Mom's Cell Phone	953-777-6789
Dad's Cell Phone	953-777-2345
Mom's Office at LLRTS	651-721-7777
Dad's Office	651-732-9909

Being prepared for an emergency is the best way to stay safe!

First Aid Kit

You can be ready for an emergency by making a first aid kit. Use a box or other container. You will need an adult to help you. First, put in a list of emergency phone numbers. Include 911 and Poison Control. Include the phone numbers for your doctor, the hospital, and a family member. Here are some good things to put in your first aid kit:

- bandages in several sizes

- medical tape

- gauze rolls and pads

- cotton balls

- latex or vinyl gloves

- safety pins

- clean tissues

- tweezers

- small scissors

- nail clippers

- hot/cold instant packs

- antibiotic ointments and creams

- hand sanitizer

- antiseptic wipes

- allergy medication like Benadryl

- pain relievers

- petroleum jelly

Books and Websites

Books

Nelson, Robin. *Playing Safely.* Minneapolis: Lerner Publications Company, 2006.

Silverstein, Alvin, Virginia Silverstein, and Laura Silverstein Nunn. *Staying Safe.* New York: Franklin Watts, 2000.

Websites

The Police Notebook: Kid Safety
http://www.ou.edu/oupd/kidsafe/kidmenu.htm

Watch Out–Kids Health for Kids
http://kidshealth.org/kid/watch/

Glossary

accidents: events that happen unexpectedly and often involve someone being hurt

ambulance: a car or truck that picks up sick or injured people and takes them to the hospital

emergency: a problem that could be dangerous and that must be dealt with quickly

first aid: care given to a sick or injured person before he or she is looked at by a doctor

injuries: cuts, scrapes, bruises, breaks, or physical harm

poisonous: harmful or dangerous if swallowed, breathed, or touched

unconscious: not awake, not able to see, feel, hear, or think

Index

Photo Acknowledgments

The photographs in this book appear courtesy of: © Todd Strand/Independent Picture Service, cover, pp. 9, 10, 15, 17, 19, 23, 25, 26; © Neal & Molly Jansen/SuperStock, p. 3; © Sam Lund/Independent Picture Service, pp. 4, 18, 22, 27; © Tom Stewart/CORBIS, p. 5; © Royalty-Free/CORBIS, p. 8; PhotoDisc Royalty Free by Getty Images, pp. 6, 11, 13; © age fotostock/SuperStock, p. 7; © Layne Kennedy/CORBIS, p. 12; © Robert Llewellyn/SuperStock, p. 14; © Mark Clarke/Photo Researchers, Inc., p. 16; © Bsip, Laurent/Photo Researchers, Inc., p. 20; © Grace/zefa/CORBIS, p. 21, © David Woods/CORBIS, p. 24.